FIRST EDITION

# GLASS CANDLESTICKS

By
## MARGARET AND DOUGLAS ARCHER

**COLLECTOR BOOKS**
*A Division of Schroeder Publishing Co., Inc.*

P.O. BOX 3009 • PADUCAH, KENTUCKY 42001

Photography
By
BRUCE H. LINKER
St. Louis, Mo.

Additional Copies of This Book May be Ordered From
COLLECTOR BOOKS
Box 3009, Paducah, Kentucky 42001
or
The Authors, MR. AND MRS. DOUGLAS ARCHER
P.O. Box 423, Ballwin, Mo. 63011

@ $7.95 Post Paid
Dealers and Clubs Write for Quantity Discounts

Printed by TAYLOR PUBLISHING COMPANY, Dallas, Texas

# Table of Contents

WE DEDICATE THIS BOOK
TO
WILMA A. SHOUSE
KERNERSVILLE, NORTH CAROLINA

# FOREWORD

The first thought in putting this book together was to apply the research which we had completed in identifying the candlesticks in our own collection. Second, if we could spare anyone some of the agony that plagued us in the identification of our sticks, we have accomplished our objective.

Our final goal was to present to you a volume on candlesticks that are available today and that can be found at a reasonable price. If a collector has enough fortitude to search and to hound the back street shops, many good pieces can be found. This, to us, is the real meaning of "collecting."

"Is it signed?" Victor Buck of Upland, California, a friend of ours once wrote, pointing out the pitfalls of today with counterfeit signatures. Why do we bring this up? Very recently a bowl and candlestick set was presented to us as signed Steuben. The items were signed in script "Steuben." The glass had applied shades of color and was cut in a well known Sinclaire Pattern. The glass had the appearance of being Steuben-made; but, with the cut, it had to be Sinclaire sold and made before 1923. The script signature was not used by Steuben until 1933. Our point is that a little research goes a long way. A piece of glass does not have to be signed to be known. Because of this, we have obtained glass candlesticks that we could never possibly afford if they had been signed — "Sleeper"? Oh yes, how sweet it is!

We could go on and on about "Sleepers" which, incidently, makes our collecting fun. But the basis for our collection did not start with "Sleepers"; it started with a gift of about forty-five (45) sticks from a very generous sister, Mrs. Wilma A. Shouse, to whom this book is dedicated. These include such items as our Sandwich Dolphin, Sandwich Milk Glass Crucifixes, Sandwich Flints, and others. Without this foundation, our collection would never have started or progressed.

With this presentation, we hope that you will find joy in the experience of identifying some of your candlesticks — as much joy as we have had in presenting them.

MARGARET AND DOUGLAS ARCHER

# ACKNOWLEDGMENTS

We hate to use the same old cliche "without their help, this book would not have been possible"; but it is a fact, and we can only thank these wonderful people from the "bottom of our hearts" for the time and consideration that they personally extended to us in putting this book together.

*We Thank You:*

Ralph Lechner
Carson, California
now
Belvidere, New Jersey .............. For the endless hours of consultation and encouragement.

Victor Buck
Upland, California ................ The foremost authority on Steuben on the West Coast, who spent hours and hours with us on Steuben and other glass.

Dr. Wilford Cohen and Dolly
Costa Mesa, California ............. Who supplied us with many sticks.

Chris Shields
Huntington Beach, California ........ For typing the countless research papers.

Everett R. Miller
Rives Junction, Michigan ............ For responding to inquiries on New Martinsville Glass.

Eleanor Spitzer
St. Louis, Missouri ................ For contributing to the collection.

Ben and Barbara Shaeffer
Costa Mesa, California ............. Who shared their glass catalogs with us.

Harold Bennett
Cambridge, Ohio .................. Who, at the Cambridge Glass Museum, consulted with us on Cambridge Glass.

John D. Hartzog and
John D. Hartzog, Jr.
Titusville, Florida . . . . . . . . . . . . . . . . . Who traded information and
catalogs with us.

Helen Warner
Williamstown, West Virginia . . . . . . . . . Of the Fenton Glass Company,
who responded to our cor-
respondence and inquiries.

Lucile J. Kennedy
Bellaire, Ohio . . . . . . . . . . . . . . . . . . . . Of the Imperial Glass Company,
who allowed us access to their
Archives and extended her
assistance in identifying
patterns of Imperial, Cambridge,
and Heisey.

Sherry Woodington
Orange, California . . . . . . . . . . . . . . . . For thoughtfulness and consideration of items and
information obtained from
her at her Antique Shop.

Nealy Cardwell
Greensboro, North Carolina . . . . . . . . . For the work on the final
draft.

And most of all,

Wilma A. Shouse
Kernersville, North Carolina . . . . . . . . . Who started the whole mess!

For those we missed, we apologize. We would like to list every
person with whom we came into contact.

# PLATE I

BOSTON AND SANDWICH GLASS COMPANY
SANDWICH, MASSACHUSETTS
1826-1888

Sandwich Candlesticks are probably the most difficult glass to find or obtain by a collector today; yet a stick will appear in very unusual places. The very rare Pink Milk Glass Crucifix (shown) was found at a Flea Market for $2.00. Many others have been viewed in the past few years, but were well out of our price range. Since little of the glass from this long established firm was signed or marked and molds were traded and copied at will during this period, it is only proper to list these candlesticks as "Attributed-To" the Boston and Sandwich Glass Company.

*TOP ROW*
  1 & 3 — CRUCIFIX — 11½ Inches High
          Pure White Milk Glass — Opaque
          Rare — (Clear Crystal more common)
      2 — CRUCIFIX — 11½ Inches High
          Milk Glass — Pink — Semi-Opaque
          Very Rare

*MIDDLE ROW*
      1 — DOLPHIN — 9½ Inches High
          Clam Broth Base — Double Square
          Applied Blue Socket

*BOTTOM ROW*
  1 & 2 — CLEAR FLINT CRYSTAL WITH PRISMS —
          10 Inches High
          Ringed Stems with Mellon
          Flared Bottom on Square Base
          Prism Ring Molded Pot Metal

(A sad note to our first plate: These sticks were destroyed when the shelves collapsed after being photographed).

# PLATE II

Butler Brothers obtained glass from the major glass houses of its day. These included: Cambridge, Fostoria, Fenton, Heisey, and Imperial. Some of the ads indicated that the glass would be shipped direct from Bellaire, Ohio (IMPERIAL) and Williamstown, West Virginia (FENTON). The glass is unidentified except for the Butler Brothers Order Numbers and the year in which they were produced.

*TOP ROW*

    1 & 2 — BUTLER NO. 1C40 — 7½ Inches High
          Butler also listed these sticks as "Colonial"

*MIDDLE ROW*

    1 & 4 — BUTLER NO. 1C38 — SMALL — 3¾ Inches High
          Better known as "Birthday Candle"
    2 & 3 — BUTLER NO. 1C38 — LARGE — 7 Inches High

*BOTTOM ROW*

    1 & 2 — GOLDEN ASSORTMENT — 7 Inches High
          In 1910 these sticks sold for $.95 a set
          (which included a matching bowl).
    3 & 4 — GOLDEN ASSORTMENT — 7 Inches High
          Cost in 1910 was $.69 each
          High quality Iridescent

# PLATE III

BUTLER BROTHERS
(Continued)

*TOP ROW*

    1 & 3 — CANDELABRA NO. 1C37 — 4½ Inches High
             Mold mark on Center Socket "Pat. Appl. For"
      2 — BUTLER NO. 1C2394 — 7½ Inches High
             1910 cost — $.33 each

*MIDDLE ROW*

    1 & 2 — HANDLED COLONIAL NO. 1C568 — 4½ Inches High
             Crystal
    3 & 4 — HANDLED COLONIAL NO. 1C568 — 4½ Inches High
             Amber
             These candlesticks were also made 5½ Inches High

*BOTTOM ROW*

    1 & 2 — HANDLED COLONIAL — 4½ Inches High
             White Milk Glass
    3 & 4 — PLAIN COLONIAL — 4½ Inches High
             White Milk Glass

             The Bottom Row of Milk Glass is shown for comparison with the Middle Row above. This Milk Glass appears to be new. Therefore, it would not carry a Butler Brothers number. Maker unknown.

# PLATE IV

CAMBRIDGE GLASS COMPANY
CAMBRIDGE, OHIO
1901-1954

> The Cambridge Glass Company made candlesticks in most of the varieties of glass that they produced. This involved forty-two (42) colors of glass. Cambridge sticks are available today for the collector with limited income with the exception of a few, such as: Rubina, Crown Tuston, Jade, Azurite, Ivory, and possibly Ebony.

*TOP ROW*

  1, 2 & 3 — NEAR-CUT WITH MATCHING BOWL —
  7 Inches High
  Pattern 200/20 — Cut 894

*MIDDLE ROW*

  1 & 3 — SHELL WITH PRISM — 7 Inches High
  Pattern No. 70
  Shell Base — ½ Satin finish
  Satin Socket

  2 — NUDE — 9 Inches High
  1935
  Pattern No. 3011
  Crystal Figure and Base
  Applied Forest Green Socket

*BOTTOM ROW*

  1 & 4 — RINGS — 8 Inches High
  Pattern 1595
  Heatherbloom — Delicate Orchid

  2 & 3 — IVORY (CUSTARD) — 9½ Inches High
  Light Cream Opaque
  Hand Enameled
  Rare if Hand Enameled is Still Intact

# PLATE V

CAMBRIDGE
(continued)

*TOP ROW*
>     1 & 2 —  TWIST — 8½ Inches High
>             Pistachio — Pastel Green

*MIDDLE ROW*
>     1, 2 & 3 —  TWIST CONSOLE SET — 8½ Inches High
>             Orange applied — Fired in Decorating Lehr

*BOTTOM ROW*
>     1 & 4 —  TWIST — 8½ Inches High
>             Satin Finish — Mandarin Gold
>     2 & 3 —  TWIST — 8½ Inches High
>             Blue Spray Enamel — Decorated and Fired in
>                 Decorating Lehr
>             (Decorations possible by Lotus — Typical of
>             their work)

# PLATE VI

CAMBRIDGE
(continued)

*TOP ROW*

    1 & 3 — CRUCIFIX — 9 Inches High
           Molded Crystal
       2 — TWO-LITE DOLPHIN — 5 Inches High
           Molded Crystal

*MIDDLE ROW*

    1 & 3 — ROSE POINT — 5 Inches High
           Pattern No. 3400-646
           Etched Rose Point Design
       2 — THREE LITE — 6 Inches High
           Pattern No. 647

*BOTTOM ROW*

    1 & 3 — CLEAR PATTERN — 7 Inches High
           Molded Crystal
       2 — MOUNT-VERNON — 8 Inches High
           Pattern No. 35
           Forest Green — Polished Socket Top

# PLATE VII

CAMBRIDGE
(Continued)

*TOP ROW*
    1 & 3 — CLASSIC — 7 Inches High
       2 — CLASSIC — 8½ Inches High
            Clear Crystal

*MIDDLE ROW*
    1 & 3 — "NEARCUT" PATTERN NO. 2862 —
            6½ Inches High
            Emerald, Clear Crystal and Clear Crystal
            with Silver Deposit

These two sticks may be confused with Duncan and Miller Pattern No. 66. The only detected difference is that the Cambridge sticks were made in 6½ Inch size, and the Duncan and Miller sticks were not. Still confusing, this stick was also made by the New Martinsville Glass Company, Pattern No. 19. The size of Pattern No. 19 is 7½ Inches High. Cambridge also made this pattern in 6½, 7 and 7½ inches.

       2 — CAMBRIDGE ARMS — 6½ Inches High
            NO. 1563-4 Candle Arm
            NO. 628 Low Candlestick

*BOTTOM ROW*
    1 & 4 — SILVER OVERLAY — 6 Inches High
            Pattern NO. 1192
            Amethyst — Dark Purple
            Base — Silver Deposit
    2 & 3 — COLONIAL — 7 Inches High
            Pattern NO. 2630

# PLATE VIII

CAMBRIDGE
(Continued)

> Cambridge sold a lot of this pattern to Lotus Glass Company of Barnesville, Ohio, who were, and still are, glass decorators.
>
> Lotus Pattern NO. 200 was one example of the use of this pattern.

*TOP ROW*
> 1 & 2 — MOONLIGHT — 8½ Inches High
> Delicate Pastel Blue

*MIDDLE ROW*
> 1 & 3 — GREEN — 7 Inches High
> Decorated Green and fired in decorating Lehr
> 2 — DELICATE PASTEL GREEN — 9½ Inches High
> Pistachio

*BOTTOM ROW*
> 1 & 4 — AMBER — 8½ Inches High
> True Amber Brown
> 2 & 3 — AMBER — 9¼ Inches High
> True Amber Brown

# PLATE IX

CENTRAL GLASS WORKS
WHEELING, WEST VIRGINIA
1860's-1939

Few candlestick patterns have been available to us on Central Glass. The only one that we have been able to identify is the "ZARICOR" pattern which was produced in 1924. Because of the "likeness" of all the sticks to the "ZARICOR" Console Set shown on PLATE X, Bottom Row, we have assumed that they are Central Glass.

*TOP ROW*

　　1 & 2 — GREEN — 9 Inches High
　　　　Small gold trim

*MIDDLE ROW*

　　1 & 2 — ORANGE — 9 Inches High
　　　　Small gold trim
　　3 & 4 — ROYAL BLUE — 9 Inches High
　　　　Small gold trim

*BOTTOM ROW*

　　1 & 2 — YELLOW — 9 Inches High
　　　　Black and gold trim
　　3 & 4 — GREEN — 9 Inches High
　　　　Black and gold trim

# PLATE X

CENTRAL GLASS WORKS
   (Continued)

*TOP ROW*
   1 & 2 — CLEAR GREEN — 7 Inches High
   3 & 4 — CLEAR AMBER — 7 Inches High

*MIDDLE ROW*
   1, 2 & 3 — RIBBED AMBER CONSOLE SET — 9 Inches High
      Base, Socket and Bowl Rim — Gold Deposit

*BOTTOM ROW*
   1, 2, 3, & 4 — ZARICOR CONSOLE SET — 9 Inches
         High with Bowl Stand

   Lotus obtained this pattern from Central Glass, decorated it and called it "MAE WEST" Pattern 200-10; Bowl and Base.

   There is a possibility that the set shown was decorated by Lotus.

# PLATE XI

CLARKE
CHILDS HILL, ENGLAND
1844-1910

Candle Lamps — Fairy Lamps — Fairy Pyramids

*TOP ROW*
    1 & 2 — HOBSTAR — 8½ Inches High (Base Only)
              Molded
              Shades new

*BOTTOM ROW*
    1 & 3 — LEAF FOOTED SATIN — 8½ Inches High
              Pink to White Satin
              Leaf applied base

These sticks cannot be truly identified. They are shown only to compare the workmanship with the Clarke Fairy Lamp. The shading, applied leaf base and the glass quality has an appearance of originating from the same source. A lot of Clarke glass was supplied by Oster of Birmingham and Thomas Webb of Stourbridge — We favor Thomas Webb in this case.

    2 — MUSHROOM FAIRY LAMP — 6¾ Inches High
           (Base only)
           Canary Yellow Satin shaded to applied White
           Satin — Leaf footed Base.
           Shade new

# PLATE XII

CZECHOSLOVAKIAN
  Location and dates unknown

> Dates and locations of this glass are difficult to establish. Most of the glass originating from this country will be signed. This is usually accomplished with a round acid etch seal "Czechoslovakia."

*TOP ROW*
  1 — BLACK GLASS — 7½ Inches High
    Signed "Czechoslovakia"
    Hand Blown with Silver applied Enamel
    (Glass is total Opaque)

*BOTTOM ROW*
  1 — CASED OVERLAY WITH PRISMS — 10 Inches
    High
    Signed "Czechoslovakia"
    White Glass with Fired Enamel over Clear Crystal
    over Cobalt Blue.
    Outer layers cut exposing Crystal and Cobalt
    Lining.

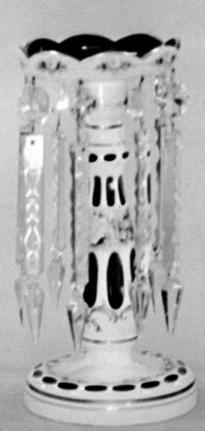

# PLATE XIII

DUNCAN AND MILLER GLASS COMPANY
WASHINGTON, PENNSYLVANIA
1865-1955 (Bought by United States Glass Company)

Duncan and Miller was best known for it's Hobnail and Early American Sandwich Patterns. The Early American Sandwich Patterns were basic copies of Boston and Sandwich glass produced in the middle 1800's. The three candlesticks shown on the Top Row are good examples of the Duncan and Miller "Sandwich" glass. These three sticks were not made by Duncan and Miller; they were made by Indiana Glass Company between 1972 and 1973. When U.S. Glass obtained the Duncan and Miller Glass Company in 1955, the "Sandwich" molds were sold to Indiana Glass Company. These three candlesticks are shown again with the Indiana Glass Company.

*TOP ROW*
- 1 & 3 — EARLY AMERICAN SANDWICH — 4 Inches High
  PATTERN NO. 41 — Clear Crystal
- 2 — EARLY AMERICAN SANDWICH — 8½ Inches High
  PATTERN NO. 41 — Amber
  (If found in clear crystal, most likely it is an original Duncan and Miller stick)

*MIDDLE ROW*
- 1 — PATTERN NO. 28 — 4 Inches High
  Clear Crystal — Silver Deposit — Socket and Base (Believed to be decorated by Lotus — Lotus NO. 202 — Grape Design)
- 2 — PATTERN NO. 28 — 6 Inches High
  Clear Crystal — Silver Deposit — Socket and Base (Believed to be decorated by Lotus — Lotus NO. 203-DEC. 889, Furiste — Modern Trend Design, Design Patent 75,974 — 1925 to 1932

*BOTTOM ROW*
- 1 & 2 — EARLY AMERICAN SANDWICH — 10 Inches High
  PATTERN NO. 141
  Pressed Crystal with removable socket
  1925-1932

# PLATE XIV

FENTON ART GLASS COMPANY
WILLIAMSTOWN, WEST VIRGINIA
1906-Present

The Fenton Art Glass Company has been producing art glass since the "Turn of the Century." The molded glass is exceptionally high grade; the free blown, outstanding. The candlesticks shown were produced around 1923 to 1930 with the exception of the bowl set shown in the Bottom Row; it was introduced in 1935.

*TOP ROW*
>   1 & 4 — JADE GREEN — 8½ Inches High
>       Pattern NO. 449
>   2 & 3 — FLORENTINE GREEN — 11½ Inches High
>       Pattern NO. 449

*MIDDLE ROW*
>   1 & 3 — GRECIAN GOLD — 8 Inches High
>       Pattern NO. 549
>   2 — AMBER DOLPHINS — 3½ Inches High
>       Pattern NO. 1623

*BOTTOM ROW*
>   1, 2, & 3 — HORN-OF-PLENTY — 5½ Inches High
>       Pattern NO. — Unknown

# PLATE XV

H. C. FRY COMPANY
ROCHESTER, PENNSYLVANIA
1901-1933
(Became a part of Libby in 1933)

The bowl set shown is FOVAL. It can be identified by the Opalescent application, changing to clear or colored shades and back to Opalescent.

1 & 3 — FOVAL STICK — 9 Inches High
2 — FOVAL BOWL — 4¾ Inches High

# PLATE XVI

## FOSTORIA GLASS COMPANY
## MOUNDSVILLE, WEST VIRGINIA
1887-Present

Fostoria started glass making in Fostoria, Ohio in 1887. This makes them the oldest single glass house operating today under the same name in the United States. Because of this, and the volume of candlesticks produced, Fostoria candlesticks are available to the Novice Collector at reasonable prices. To this day, we have not seen a candlestick by Fostoria that we didn't like.

*TOP ROW*
1 & 2 — PATTERN NO. 1963 — 9 Inches High
Introduced 1920 — Discontinued 1925
(Identical to New Martinsville Pattern
10-21 Forest Green)

*MIDDLE ROW*
1 & 2 — PATTERN NO. 2245 — 8 Inches High
Introduced 1924 — Discontinued 1928

*BOTTOM ROW*
1 & 2 — ORLEANS DESIGN — 2 Inches High
Pattern NO. 2394
Introduced 1929 — Discontinued 1930
Light Green

# PLATE XVII

FOSTORIA
(Continued)

*TOP ROW*

    1 & 3 — PATTERN NO. 2535 — 5½ Inches High
               Introduced in 1936
               Discontinued in 1944
       2 — PATTERN NO. 2527 — 8½ Inches High
               2527 Bobeshe missing

*MIDDLE ROW*

    1 & 3 — PATTERN NO. 2395 — 3 Inches High
               Amber
       2 — PATTERN NO. 2395½ — 5 Inches High
               Versailles Design
               Plate Etching No. 278
               Design Patent No. 76,372 and 76,454
               Topaz

*BOTTOM ROW*

    1 & 3 — BAROQUE — PATTERN — 4 Inches High
               No. 2496 Line
       2 — BAROQUE — PATTERN — 5½ Inches High
               2496 Line
               Corsage Design
               Plate Etching No. 325
               Introduced 1935 — Discontinued 1960

# PLATE XVIII

A. H. HEISEY AND COMPANY
301 OAKWOOD AVENUE
NEWARK, OHIO
1893-1956

Heisey glass was known for its brilliant fire-polished, hand-molded crystal. Although the Company was founded in 1893, the famous "Diamond H" Trade Mark did not appear until the fall of 1900. The mark was registered in August, 1901. Few early (1893 — 1900) candlesticks were marked, but the standard use of "Punted Bottom," as described in Heisey Catalogs, indicated a polished pontil which is usually distinguishable. All sticks shown, except for the "Flutes," have a "Punted Bottom." Unless indicated, they were made between 1893 and 1900.

*TOP ROW*

1 — FLUTE WITH HANDLE — PATTERN NO. 32 —
7¼ Inches High
Applied Handle
2 — FLUTE — PLAIN — 5¼ Inches High
Date Unknown

*MIDDLE ROW*

1 — PATTERN NO. 2-300 — 9 Inches High
2 — PATTERN NO. 4 — 9½ Inches High

*BOTTOM ROW*

1 & 2 — AMBER CUT — 10 Inches High
The Socket and Tear Drop Center is "Wheel Cut"
Amber — After 1900

# PLATE XVIX

HEISEY
(Continued)

*TOP ROW*

    1 — RIBBED — 9¼ Inches High
            Date Unknown
    2 — TROPHY — 9¼ Inches High
            Date Unknown
    3 — PATTERN NO. 134 — 5½ Inches High
            This pattern first appeared around 1925 as
            Heisey sold it to Lotus. Lotus decorated
            it as Pattern No. 39 — Twin Light. Heisey
            was still producing the pattern in the
            early 1950's.

*MIDDLE ROW*

    1 & 4 — COLONIAL — 6¼ Inches High
            After 1905
    2 & 3 — PATTERN NO. 300 — 7 Inches High
            This stick was also made in 9 Inches and was
            one of the few cut pieces of glass made by
            Heisey between 1893 and 1900.

*BOTTOM ROW*

    1 — NO. 1401 EMPRESS — 6 Inches High
            Wheel Engraved Pattern 135
            After 1930
    2 & 3 — BOX SWIRL — 9¾ Inches High
            "Diamond-H" Mold Marked ater 1920
    4 — CRYSTAL — 8 Inches High
            Date unknown

# PLATE XX

HEISEY
(Continued)

1 & 3 — PATTERN NO. 5 TOY — 6½ Inches High
2 — PATTERN NO. 5 — 11 Inches High
Heisey also made Pattern No. 5 in a 9 Inch stick

# PLATE XXI

IMPERIAL GLASS COMPANY
BELLAIRE, OHIO
1901-Present

From pressed glass to engraved glass — you name it, Imperial has made it. This includes candlesticks from all Eras of the Company. A good cross section is shown on the following Plates with the exception of Imperial art glass which we do not have. To add to the depth and variety of the Company's lines, in 1940, Imperial acquired Central Glass Works of Wheeling, West Virginia. In 1958 Imperial acquired the famous molds of Cambridge and Heisey. Candlesticks from these molds are being produced today. Imperial is now owned by Lenox, Inc.

*TOP ROW*

1 — PATTERN NO. 352 — 7½ Inches High
1973
Obtained from the Flemming Glass Company
Flemmington, New Jersey
Opaque — Caramel Slag

2 — VIKING ROCK CRYSTAL — PATTERN NO. 753
— 7 Inches High
1932

3 — PATTERN NO. 352 — 7½ Inches High
1920 Clear — "NU-CUT"

*MIDDLE ROW*

1 & 2 — EMPIRE DOLPHIN — 9 Inches High
1925-1935 — Light Blue

3 — IMPERIAL DOLPHIN — 9 Inches High
1974 (A reward of my visit to the Imperial
Factory, October, 1974)

4 & 5 — EMPIRE DOLPHIN — PATTERN NO. 779 —
5 Inches High
1925-1935 — Clear

*BOTTOM ROW*

1 & 3 — "NEWBOUND" — PATTERN NO. 153B —
4½ Inches High
1925-1935 — Ritz Blue

2 — PATTERN NO. 637 — 3½ Inches High
1925-1935
True Pink — Gold Overlay

# PLATE XXII

IMPERIAL
(Continued)

*TOP ROW*
    1 & 2 — SPECIAL LOT PATTERN NO. 41 — 7 Inches High
        Originally produced 1920-1930

*MIDDLE ROW*
    1 — PATTERN NO. 419 — 9 Inches High
        Amethyst — 1920
    2 — PATTERN NO. 419 — 9 Inches High
        Iridescent to Clear Crystal — 1920

*BOTTOM ROW*
    1 & 4 — PATTERN NO. 635 — 8½ Inches High
        1920-1930
        Amethyst — Sterling Silver Overlay
    2 — PATTERN NO. 635 — 8½ Inches High
        1920-1930
        Iridescent
    3 — PATTERN NO. 635 — 8½ Inches High
        1920 — 1930
        Pale Green

# PLATE XXIII

INDIANA GLASS COMPANY
DUNKIRK, INDIANA
1907-Present

In Plate XIII we explored the relation between Indiana Glass Company and Duncan and Miller Glass Company. The listing of the Bottom Row again is for the benefit of the identification of the maker of the glass and not the molds. It is our understanding that Indiana Glass Company is only producing the Early American Pattern No. 170 in Amber and not in Clear Crystal as the original sticks were produced. At this writing, we have not investigated the colors involving Sandwich Pattern NO. 41. We bought the pair new in 1973, it being the only color available from the source. The one piece of old Indiana Glass is so beautiful we wish that we had more of it.

*TOP ROW*

1 — GARLAND — NO. 301 Line — 5½ Inches High
Hand-made — Fire-Polished
1935

*BOTTOM ROW*

1 & 3 — SANDWICH — PATTERN NO. 41 — 4 Inches High
1973
2 — EARLY AMERICAN — PATTERN NO. 170 —
8¼ Inches High
1973

# PLATE XXIV

JEANNETTE GLASS COMPANY
JEANNETTE, PENNSYLVANIA
1900-Present

*TOP ROW*

    1 & 3 —   PATTERN NO. 26 — 7 Inches High
              1926
              Amber
      2 —     PATTERN NO. 26 — 7 Inches High
              1915-1918
              Clear Crystal — Sunturned

*MIDDLE ROW*

1, 2, 3, 4 & 5 —   PATTERN NO. X-31 — 6½ Inches High
              Clear Crystal
              Blue — Fired
              Orange — Fired
              Clear Crystal with applied flower decorations
              (Decorations do not appear to be fired)
              1924

*BOTTOM ROW*

    1, 2 & 3 —   IRIS PATTERN — 5½ Inches High
              Made between 1928 — 1932 with the exception of
              the Clear Crystal which was made between 1950-
              1969.

              Frosted
              Clear Crystal
              Iridescent

# PLATE XXV

LANCASTER GLASS COMPANY
LANCASTER, OHIO
1908-1937
1937-Present (Plant #2, Anchor Hocking Corporation)

*TOP ROW*
    1 & 3 — PATTERN NO. 854 — 3 Inches High
            1925-1931
            Medium Green
       2 — PATTERN NO. R-1830 — 1½ Inches High
            1925-1931

*MIDDLE ROW*
    1 & 3 — PATTERN NO. 83 — 8¼ and 8½ Inches High
            1924
            Light Green and Medium Green
       2 — PATTERN NO. 83 — 8½ Inches High
            1924
            Amber

*BOTTOM ROW*
        PATTERN NO. 83 — 8½ Inches High

Matching candlesticks and Candy Bowl 1924 — Advertisement indicated this Satin Glass was available for cutting and decorating. This set could have been decorated by some other company. Interesting note: sticks were found in Orange County, California. The matching candy bowl was a gift from a friend in Ladue, Missouri.

# PLATE XXVI

McKEE GLASS COMPANY
JEANNETTE, PENNSYLVANIA
1853-1888 McKee & Bros. — Pittsburgh
1888-1903 McKee & Bros. — Jeannette
1903-1951 McKee Glass Co. — Jeanette
1951-1961 Thatcher Glass Co. — McKee Division
1961-Present Jeanette Glass Corporation

Out of tons and tons of McKee Glass made, few candlesticks were included in their patterns. If you have a known McKee stick, consider it rare.

*TOP ROW*
1 — VULCAN DESIGN — 6 Inches High
1920-1930
2 — SMALL CRUCIFIX — 9 Inches High
1910-1930
Light Green

*BOTTOM ROW*
1 & 2 — RAY — 8 Inches High
Clear Crystal
1910-1930

When we first saw these sticks, we were sure we had found a pair of "BACCARAT." Now that we have been able to identify them, "Good Ole McKee is good enough for me."

# PLATE XXVII

MEISSEN / DRESDEN
ROYAL SAXON PORCELAIN WORKS
MEISSEN, GERMANY
Established 1710

Although these candlesticks are not glass, we feel they should be identified to explain the mis-use of the term "Meissen" and "Dresden." Since Meissen, Germany, is only a few miles from Dresden, Germany, somewhere along the line Meissen Porcelain became known as "Dresden." The term "Dresden" for Meissen originated in England and eventually spread to America. Around 1850 the Meissen Works shipped large quantities of unpromoted "Dresden" to America unsigned. This is the Meissen which is mostly available today.

1 — BOY WITH HORN-OF-PLENTY — 10 ⅝ Inches
      High
      Porcelain — Hard Paste
      "Horn-Of-Plenty" Socket has Metal Liner
2 — CANDELABRA — 13 ¾ Inches High
      Porcelain — Hard Paste
      Candelabra removable from base

# PLATE XXVIII

NEW MARTINSVILLE GLASS
MANUFACTURING COMPANY
NEW MARTINSVILLE, WEST VIRGINIA
1901-1944
1944-Present — Viking Glass Company

*TOP ROW*
    1 & 2 — PATTERN NO. 415 — 6½ Inches High
                     1937-1944

*MIDDLE ROW*
    1 & 3 — PATTERN NO. 10 — 4 Inches High
                     Crystal Flute with Handle
                     1901-1937
       2 — PATTERN NO. 10 — 4 Inches High
                     Crystal Flute without Handle
                     1901-1937

*BOTTOM ROW*
    1 & 3 — VOGUE PATTERN NO. 4554/401 — 5 Inches High
                     1937-1944
       2 — PATTERN NO. 18 — 6 Inches High
                     1937-1944

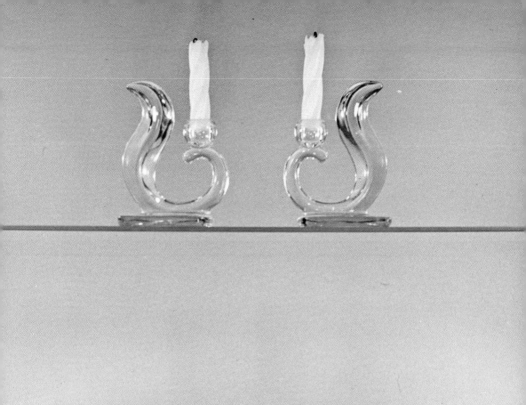

# PLATE XXIX

NEW MARTINSVILLE
(Continued)

*TOP ROW*
>    1 & 2 — PATTERN NO. 169 — 7 Inches High
>        1901-1937

*MIDDLE ROW*
>    1 & 2 — PATTERN NO. 14 — 7 Inches High
>        Sterling Silver Overlay
>        1901-1937

*BOTTOM ROW*
>    1 & 3 —COLONIAL — PATTERN NO. 11 — 5½ Inches High
>        1901-1937
>        2 — PATTERN NO. 19 — 7½ Inches High
>        Purple Fried Enamel

# PLATE XXX

PAIRPOINT GLASS COMPANY
NEW BEDFORD, MASSACHUSETTS
Since 1968 — Sagamore, Mass.

*TOP ROW*

      1 — AIR-TWIST — 9⅝ Inches High
          Four (4) Air Twists
          Clear Crystal — Cut Socket

*MIDDLE ROW*

      1 — SWIRL BALL — 4 Inches High
          Blue applied Socket and Base
          Swirl clear ball center
          (Typical of Pairpoints "Ball Design"
          objects. These balls come in clear,
          swirl and, most common, air bubbles.)
      2 — BELL TOP — 7½ Inches High
          Light Amethyst — Cut Socket
      3 — SILVER BASE — 5 Inches High
          Bell Top
          Heavy Silver Overlay on Rim Base
          Ball feet — Silver

*BOTTOM ROW*

    1, 2 & 3 — AMBER BOWL SET
          Candlesticks — 3½ Inches High
          Bowl — 4¾ Inches High

# PLATE XXXI

PEKING GLASS WORKS
PEKING, CHINA
Late 1800's

Little information is available on Peking Glass. It is known that the Peking Glass Works made Contract Glass for the American market. Since the "Cock" is a symbol of power in China, it is believed that the "Cock's Foot" sticks, shown, are the original metal with the glass. The Dragon is similar metal and casting. It is assumed that it is from the same source.

*TOP ROW*

    1 — COCK'S FOOT AND LEG — 5 Inches High
        Cast Metal
    2 — DRAGON — 5½ Inches High
        Cast Metal

*MIDDLE ROW*

    1 — COCK'S FOOT — EGG CENTER — 6 Inches High
        Pastel Blue Milk Glass — Opaque
    2 — COCK'S FOOT — EGG CENTER — 6 Inches High
        Pastel Green Milk Glass — Opaque

*BOTTOM ROW*

    1 — COCK'S FOOT — GLASS CENTER — 5½ Inches High
        Yellow Milk Glass — Opaque
        Poor quality
    2 — OAK LEAVES WITH GLASS — 7½ Inches High
        Pastel Blue Milk Glass — Cased — Opaque
        Cast Metal Base in shape of Oak Leaves
    3 — COCK'S FOOT AND GLASS — 5½ Inches High
        Pink Tripled Cased Glass — Opaque

# PLATE XXXII

PORTIEUX
PORTIEUX, FRANCE
Operation Date Unknown

No information is available on this glass house. The glass shown was produced between 1900 and 1920. The glass is marked in "mold relief" — "PORTIEUX."

*TOP ROW*

1 — MONK — 9½ Inches High
Monk Frosted
Base and Socket Clear
Base has four Angel Faces with Wings in Relief.

*BOTTOM ROW*

1 & 2 — DRUNK AROUND LAMP POST — 10 Inches High
Drunk and Lamp post Frosted
Base and Socket Clear
Base has Grape Design in Relief

# PLATE XXXIII

ROSENTHAL
Germany

No research was done on Rosenthal Glass. Rosenthal is still producing very fine crystal — which today can be found in better glass shops or department stores. Although Rosenthal makes fine engraved crystal, the hand-free blown sticks shown are typical of their quality. All Rosenthal glass will be acid marked with an "R" and a Crown over the "R".

We are most grateful for this one pair of sticks — Thanks to a friend in Ladue, Missouri.

1 — ROSENTHAL TULIPS — 15½ Inches High
  Hand Blown —
  Smoke Gray Socket
  Clear Crystal Stem & Base

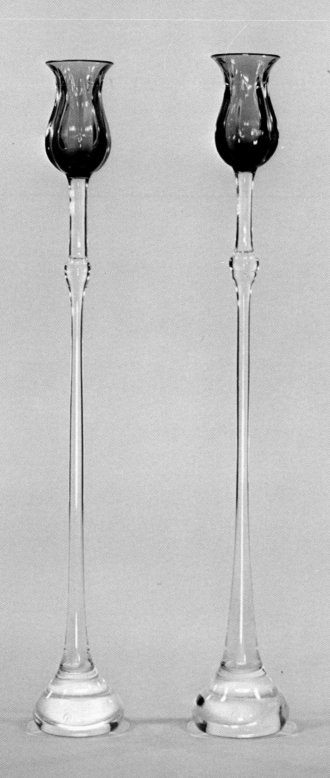

# PLATE XXXIV

## L. E. SMITH GLASS COMPANY
## MT. PLEASANT, PENNSYLVANIA
### 1907-Present

Lewis E. Smith came and went, only spending a few short years in the glass business. Smith candlesticks are about as hard to find as Mr. Smith himself. Known for its Black Glass in the 30's, the Black pair shown represent the fine quality of products produced during this period.

*TOP ROW*

1 & 2 — MOUNT PLEASANT — PATTERN NO. 600 —
    4½ Inches High
    Black Glass
    If found in Blue — Very rare
    Also called "Do-Si-Do"
    1930's

*MIDDLE ROW*

1 & 2 — CRYSTAL MOLDED WITH PRISMS —
    8½ Inches High
    A take-off of Pattern No. 1/18
    1930

*BOTTOM ROW*

1 & 4 — PATTERN NO. 805 — 3½ Inches High
    Pink — Gold Overlay with wheel Cuttings

2 & 3 — CRUCIFIX — 9 Inches High
    Gold Decorated
    Clear Crystal
    1922-1926
    (This is the only pair of Smith Crucifix
    Candlesticks we have ever seen. The Gold
    is one of the keys to identification of these
    sticks).

# PLATE XXXV

## HENRY P. SINCLAIRE COMPANY
## CORNING, NEW YORK

"Shades" of Hawkes and Steuben: This is may first thought when I find a candlestick by Sinclaire. Why do I think this? H. P. Sinclaire was a director of the T. G. Hawkes Company of Corning which was a co-founder of Steuben. Sinclaire obtained blanks from Steuben and Hawkes for cutting. Glass blown by Sinclaire had a Steuben flare. All glass shown was made before 1923.

*TOP ROW*

1 — BLUE COLUMN — 12 Inches High
Sinclaire Blue with applied "Knots"
Rolled Rim Base and Bobeche
Rough Pontil

2 — BLUE HOUR-GLASS — 12¼ Inches High
Slight Twist in "Hour-Glass" Stem
Rolled Rim Base
Rough Pontil

*MIDDLE ROW*

1 — CRYSTAL — 10¼ Inches High
Cut, Acid or Fire Polished, Final Cut
Flowers on Stem and Socket
Star Pattern cut on bottom of Base
(Glass believed to be Steuben made)

*BOTTOM ROW*

1, 2, & 3 — YELLOW GRAPE SET — 10⅝ Inches High (Sticks)
4¾ Inches High (Bowl)
Fine Wheel Cut Bunches of Grapes and Grape
Leaves, Grape Leaves on Base
Rough Pontil — (glass believed to be Steuben made)

# PLATE XXXVI

STEUBEN GLASS COMPANY
CORNING, NEW YORK
1903-1918
1918-Present — Steuben Division
             Corning Glass Company

We could really get wound up over Frederick Carter Glass and words about Carter himself, but that's not the purpose of this book. Our purpose is to show an example of Steuben Candlesticks that can be found today at a reasonable price.

CAUTION: Do not expect to find signed Steuben sticks at a reasonable price. You will not. If in doubt about a piece of glass — and the price is right — buy it. Research it: if it turns out to be Steuben, you will find it was worth it. We had an unfair advantage with this approach by having Victor Buck of Upland, California, to consult with. For the time he spent with us and the little things about Steuben he taught us, we will always be grateful.

*TOP ROW*

1 — PATTERN NO. 6505 — 14 Inches High
Light Blue with Bubble Patterns in Glass
Threaded Ball Stem and Bobeche
Rolled Rim Base — Rough Pontil

2 — PATTERN NO. 6043 — 12 Inches High
Blue stem — Air Flicked
Applied Base and Socket in Amber Twist
Rolled Rim — Rough Pontil

*BOTTOM ROW*

1 — PATTERN NO. 2940 — 8 Inches High
Amethyst Twist Stem
Applied Amber Base and Socket

2 & 3 — PATTERN NO. 2956 — 12 Inches High
Amber
Rolled Rim Base — Rough Pontil

4 — PATTERN NO. 6384 — 4 Inches High
Medium Green
Rolled Rim Base — Rough Pontil

# PLATE XXXVII

UNITED STATES GLASS COMPANY
Now Known as — "TIFFIN"
1891-Present — The Interpace Corporation
Tiffin, Ohio

Where to start with U.S. Glass is difficult. With 18 glass factories at one time, anyone could have made a pattern at any factory at any time. Confusing? The whole history of U.S. Glass is confusing. We have tried to unravel the sticks that we believe to be either a U.S. Glass product or a "Tiffin" product.

*TOP ROW*
1 & 2 — PATTERN NO. 15319 — 8 Inches High
Ink Stain Coloring
Baluster Design
Sticks from a three piece Console Set
1924

*MIDDLE ROW*
1, 2 & 3 — ELYSIUM — 2 Inches High
Green and Satin Blue with Decoration
1926

*BOTTOM ROW*
1, 2 & 3 — BLACK TIFFIN GLASS — 9 Inches High — Sticks
5½ Inches High — Bowl
No additional information available

# PLATE XXXVII

VENETIAN
Area of Murano, Italy
Dates Unknown

> Venetian Glass, as it is called, may come from a variety of places. The fine Arts Glass generally originated from the Island of Murano not too far from Venice. Fine glass from this area was known to exist in the Fifteenth and Sixteenth Century. The articles shown are not very old.

*TOP ROW*

1 — DOLPHINS — 14¾ Inches High
Ribbed Stim with Gold Fleck Dolphins — Applied with Gold Fleck Amber applied Socket and Base — Quilted Base has Rolled Rim — Rough Pontil (Except for the applied Dolphins, the quality of this stick would tend to appear as a Steuben or Sinclaire).

*BOTTOM ROW*

1 — DOLPHIN — 6½ Inches High
Dolphin Stem with Gold Fleck
Swirl Base and Socket with Gold Fleck
Base has Rolled Rim — Rough Pontil

2 — ROSES — 4 Inches High
Pewter Leaves with Porcelain Roses
(A gift from a very Dear Friend)

3 — VASA MURRHINA — 10 Inches High
Combination of Spatter and Aventurine
Crystal cased

# PLATE XXXIX

WESTMORELAND GLASS COMPANY
Formerly — WESTMORELAND SPECIALITY COMPANY
GRAPEVILLE, PENNSYLVANIA
1891-Present

When speaking of Westmoreland Candlesticks, one usually will start with the "Dolphins," maybe get around to the "Wakefield" but most likely will end up with the "Dolphins." That's about what we do here.

*TOP ROW*

1 — PATTERN NO. 1049 DOLPHIN — 4 Inches High
1924
Pink

2 & 3 — PATTERN NO. 1049 MILK GLASS DOLPHIN —
4 Inches High
(Believed to be new pattern)
Date Unknown

*BOTTOM ROW*

1 & 2 — CRYSTAL DOLPHIN — 9¼ Inches High
1925

Because of these candlestick's fine quality, they are probably the most mis-represented Dolphins found today. We have ssen them marked Heisey, Fostoria and even Boston and Sandwich. It is not known to us that anyone else copied or made this base.

# PLATE XXXX

WESTMORELAND
(Continued)

*TOP ROW*

    1 — LOTUS — SATIN AMBER — 3¾ Inches High
    Originally made 1924—1926
    This one — New 1972
    (Gift from a Friend in North Carolina)

*MIDDLE ROW*

    1 — CLEAR WITH ORANGE AND BLACK —
        9 Inches High
    Added Decorations on Base
    1924-1926
    (All added Decorations appear to be similar)
    2 — PATTERN NO. 1803 — GREEN SATIN —
        9 Inches High
    Added Decorations on Base
    1924-1926
    3 — PINK WITH BLACK BASE — 9 Inches High
    Added Decorations on Base
    1924-1926

*BOTTOM ROW*

    1 & 3 — PATTERN NO. 1803 — 9 Inches High
    Blue with Black and Gold Trim — Fired
    1924-1926
    2 — PATTERN NO. 1803 — 9 Inches High
    Blue with Black Trim Enamel — Fired
    1924-1926

# PLATE XXXXI

POT 'POURRI

*TOP ROW*

      1 — FEDERAL'S FLUTE — 4 Inches High
           1920-1930
           Federal Glass Company
           Columbus, Ohio
           1900-Present

*MIDDLE ROW*

      1 — GREENSBURG'S PATTERN 1402 — 3 Inches High
           Greensburg Glass Works
           Greensburg, Pennsylvania
           (During 1920-1930 — Acquired by L. E. Smith)
      2 — HAZEL ATLAS DOLPHIN — 7½ Inches High
           Hazel Atlas Glass Company
           Wheeling, West Virginia
           1902-Present
           Dolphins 1930's

*BOTTOM ROW*

      1 — GORHAM'S "THE TWILIGHT — PATENTED"
           — 11½ Inches High
           Candlestick Oil Lamp
           Anchor Seal and Half Moon Imprint also
           1733/3
           Milk Glass Oil Holder
           (Candlestick Unknown)

# PLATE XXXXII

POT'POURRI

*TOP ROW*

    1 — PADEN CITY CRYSTAL — 3½ Inches High
        PADEN CITY GLASS MANUFACTURING
          COMPANY
        PADEN CITY, WEST VIRGINIA
        1916-1951
        (Pattern same as 191 Line without ridges)
        Believed to be made before 1928
    2 — PHOENIX RELIEF — 3½ Inches High
        PHOENIX GLASS COMPANY
        BEAVER COUNTY, PENNSYLVANIA
        Dates Unknown
        Believed to be in 1930's

*MIDDLE ROW*

    1, 2, & 3 — ROSEVILLE POTTERY
             ZANESVILLE, OHIO
        The set shown is typical of the Roseville Designs. All
        Roseville Sticks that I have seen are mold signed. This
        set was a gift from my Son and Daughter-in-Law and
        was found in Cheyenne, Wyoming.
        Pattern 1156 — 2½ Inches High

*BOTTOM ROW*

    1, 2, & 3 — WILLIAMSBURG POTTERY
             WILLIAMSBURG, VIRGINIA
        SOFT BISQUE
        Light Tan with Blue Flowers
        1960
        Last but not least — This is the first set of
        sticks we ever owned.

# CRUCIFIXES

# DOLPHINS

95

# UNKNOWNS

98

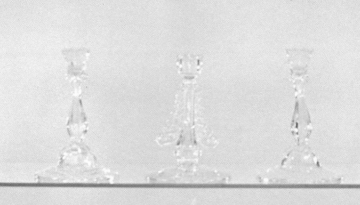

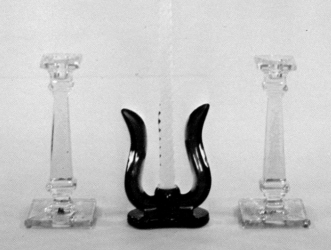

# UNKNOWNS

# UNKNOWNS

# PRICE GUIDE

To try to establish a price guide that would average-out for any selection of the country, we have listed what we feel is a low or more true value, of what a candlestick should sell for, and a high, representing the maximum that we feel, it is worth.

### PLATE I
*TOP ROW*
| | | | |
|---|---|---|---|
| 1 & 3 — CRUCIFIX .................... | 600.00-700.00 | Pair |
| 2 — Crucifix ...................... | 250.00-300.00 | Single |

*MIDDLE ROW*
| | | | |
|---|---|---|---|
| 1 — DOLPHIN.................... | 175.00-200.00 | Single |

*BOTTOM ROW*
| | | | |
|---|---|---|---|
| 1 & 2 — FLINTS ...................... | 300.00-350.00 | Pair |

### PLATE II
*TOP ROW*
| | | | |
|---|---|---|---|
| 1 & 2 — No. 1C40 .................... | 25.00-30.00 | Pair |

*MIDDLE ROW*
| | | | |
|---|---|---|---|
| 1 & 4 — No. 1C38S .................... | 18.00-22.00 | Pair |
| 2 & 3 — No. 1C38L .................... | 26.00-30.00 | Pair |

*BOTTOM ROW*
| | | | |
|---|---|---|---|
| 1 & 2 — GOLDEN ASSORTMENT......... | 24.00-28.00 | Pair |
| 1 & 2 — GOLDEN ASSORTMENT......... | 28.00-32.00 | Pair |

### PLATE III
*TOP ROW*
| | | | |
|---|---|---|---|
| 1 & 3 — CANDELABRA................. | 26.00-30.00 | Pair |
| 2 — No. 1C2394 .................... | 20.00-22.00 | Single |

*MIDDLE ROW*
| | | | |
|---|---|---|---|
| 1 & 2 — No. 1C568 .................... | 15.00-18.00 | Pair |
| 3 & 4 — No. 1C568 .................... | 17.00-20.00 | Pair |

*BOTTOM ROW*
Priced to be new
| | | | |
|---|---|---|---|
| 1 & 2 — HANDLED COLONIAL ......... | 4.00-6.00 | Pair |
| 3 & 4 — PLAIN COLONIAL ............. | 5.00-6.00 | Pair |

### PLATE IV
*TOP ROW*
| | | | |
|---|---|---|---|
| 1, 2 & 3 — NEAR-CUT SET ................ | 40.00-43.00 | Set |

*MIDDLE ROW*
| | | | |
|---|---|---|---|
| 1 & 3 — SHELL WITH PRISM............ | 32.00-36.00 | Pair |
| 2 — NUDE ...................... | 50.00-55.00 | Single |

*BOTTOM ROW*
| | | | |
|---|---|---|---|
| 1 & 4 — RINGS....................... | 28.00-32.00 | Pair |
| 2 & 3 — IVORY (Plain) .................. | 60.00-70.00 | Pair |
| With Decorations ................ | 100.00-125.00 | Pair |

### PLATE V
*TOP ROW*
| | | | |
|---|---|---|---|
| 1 & 2 — TWIST ...................... | 40.00-45.00 | Pair |

*MIDDLE ROW*
| | | | |
|---|---|---|---|
| 1, 2, & 3 — TWIST CONSOLE SET .......... | 28.00-30.00 | Set |

*BOTTOM ROW*
| | | | |
|---|---|---|---|
| 1 & 4 — TWIST ...................... | 45.00-50.00 | Pair |
| 2 & 3 — TWIST ...................... | 35.00-40.00 | Pair |

## PLATE VI

*TOP ROW*

    1 & 3 — CRUCIFIX ...................... 25.00-35.00 Pair

    2 — TWO-LITE DOLPHIN ........... 18.00-24.00 Single

*MIDDLE ROW*

    1 & 3 — ROSE POINT ................... 30.00-34.00 Pair

    2 — THREE-LITE ................... 18.00-20.00 Single

*BOTTOM ROW*

    1 & 3 — CLEAR PATTERN .............. 20.00-24.00 Pair

    2 — MOUNT VERNON .............. 27.00-32.00 Pair

## PLATE VII

*TOP ROW*

    1 & 3 — CLASSIC ...................... 36.00-40.00 Pair

    2 — CLASSIC ...................... 28.00-36.00 Single

*MIDDLE ROW*

    1, 2, & 3 — PATTERN NO. 2862 ............. 7.00-9.00 Each

*BOTTOM ROW*

    1 & 4 — SILVER OVERLAY .............. 42.00-48.00 Pair

    2 & 3 — COLONIAL ................... 45.00-50.00 Pair

## PLATE VIII

*TOP ROW*

    1 & 2 — MOONLIGHT .................. 40.00-45.00 Pair

*MIDDLE ROW*

    1 & 3 — GREEN ......................... 28.00-30.00 Pair

    2 — DELICATE PASTEL GREEN...... 18.00-20.00 Single

*BOTTOM ROW*

    1 & 4 — AMBER ........................ 40.00-45.00 Pair

    2 & 3 — AMBER ........................ 45.00-50.00 Pair

## PLATE IX

*TOP ROW*

    1 & 2 — GREEN ........................ 15.00-18.00 Pair

*MIDDLE ROW*

    1 & 2 — ORANGE ...................... 15.00-18.00 Pair

    3 & 4 — ROYAL BLUE ................... 15.00-18.00 Pair

*BOTTOM ROW*

    1 & 2 — YELLOW ...................... 18.00-20.00 Pair

    3 & 4 — GREEN ........................ 18.00-20.00 Pair

## PLATE X

*TOP ROW*

    1 & 2 — GLEAR GREEN ................. 12.00-14.00 Pair

    3 & 4 — CLEAR AMBER ................ 12.00-14.00 Pair

*MIDDLE ROW*

    1, 2 & 3 — RIBBED AMBER CONSOLE SET .. 45.00-60.00 Set

*BOTTOM ROW*

    1, 2, 3, & 4 — ZARICON CONSOLE SET ........ 48.00-58.00 Set

## PLATE XI

*TOP ROW*

    1 & 2 — HOBSTAR (Base only) ........... 50.00-56.00 Pair

    With Shades — OLD ............ 125.00-150.00 Pair

*BOTTOM ROW*

    1 & 3 — LEAF FOOTED SATIN ........... 100.00-130.00 Pair

    2 — MUSHROOM FAIRY LAMB ...... 130.00-150.00 Single

    With Shade — OLD ............. 300.00-350.00

## PLATE XII

*TOP ROW*

    1 — BLACK GLASS .................      27.00-32.00   Single

*BOTTOM ROW*

    1 — CASED OVERLAY WITH PRISMS      130.00-150.00   Single

## PLATE XIII

*TOP ROW*

    SEE INDIANA GLASS PLATE XXIII

*MIDDLE ROW*

    1 — PATTERN 28-4″ .................      28.00-32.00   Single
    2 — PATTERN 28-6″ .................      32.00-36.00   Single

*BOTTOM ROW*

    1 & 2 — EARLY AMERICAN SANDWICH .      50.00-60.00   Pair

## PLATE XIV

*TOP ROW*

    1 & 4 — JADE GREEN ...................      30.00-35.00   Pair
    2 & 3 — FLORENTINE GREEN ..........      60.00-70.00   Pair

*MIDDLE ROW*

    1 & 3 — GRECIAN GOLD ...............      45.00-55.00   Pair
    2 — AMBER DOLPHINS .............      12.00-14.00   Single

*BOTTOM ROW*

    1, 2 & 3 — HORN-OF-PLENTY ..............      30.00-34.00   Set

## PLATE XV

    1, 2 & 3 — FOVAL SET ....................      100.00-130.00   Set

## PLATE XVI

*TOP ROW*

    1 & 2 — PATTERN NO. 1963 ..............      36.00-40.00   Pair

*MIDDLE ROW*

    1 & 2 — PATTERN NO. 2245 ..............      18.00-20.00   Pair

*BOTTOM ROW*

    1 & 2 — ORLEANS DESIGN ..............      10.00-12.00   Pair

## PLATE XVII

*TOP ROW*

    1 & 3 — PATTERN 2535 .................      8.00-10.00   Pair
    2 — PATTERN 2527 as is ..............      7.00-9.00   Single

*MIDDLE ROW*

    1 & 3 — PATTERN NO. 2395 ..............      14.00-16.00   Pair
    2 — PATTERN NO. 2395½ Etched ......      9.00-11.00   Single

*BOTTOM ROW*

    1 & 3 — BAROQUE .....................      16.00-18.00   Pair
    2 — BAROQUE .....................      10.00-12.00   Single

## PLATE XVIII

*TOP ROW*

    1 — FLUTE WITH HANDLE..........      45.00-60.00   Single
    2 — FLUTE — PLAIN ...............      38.00-47.00   Single

*MIDDLE ROW*

    1 — PATTERN 2-300 .................      65.00-70.00   Single
    2 — PATTERN 4 ....................      50.00-60.00   Single

*BOTTOM ROW*

    1 & 2 — AMBER CUT ...................      120.00-130.00   Pair

## PLATE XXIX

TOP ROW

| | | |
|---|---|---|
| 1 — RIBBED | 40.00-45.00 | Single |
| 2 — TROPHY | 45.00-50.00 | Single |
| 3 — PATTERN 134 | 10.00-12.00 | Single |

MIDDLE ROW

| | | |
|---|---|---|
| 1 & 4 — COLONIAL | 65.00-70.00 | Pair |
| 2 & 3 — PATTERN 300 | 90.00-100.00 | Pair |

BOTTOM ROW

| | | |
|---|---|---|
| 1 — NO. 1401 EMPRESS | 8.00-10.00 | Single |
| 2 & 3 — BOX SWIRL | 60.00-70.00 | Pair |
| 4 — CRYSTAL | 28.00-30.00 | Single |

## PLATE XX

| | | |
|---|---|---|
| 1 & 3 — PATTERN 5 TOY | 40.00-48.00 | Pair |
| 2 — PATTERN 5 (Stick only) | 85.00-100.00 | Single |

## PLATE XXI

TOP ROW

| | | |
|---|---|---|
| 1 — PATTERN 352 | 12.00-14.00 | Single |
| 2 — VIKING ROCK CRYSTAL | 16.00-18.00 | Single |
| 3 — PATTERN 352 | 28.00-34.00 | Single |

MIDDLE ROW

| | | |
|---|---|---|
| 1 & 2 — EMPIRE DOLPHIN | 18.00-22.00 | Pair |
| 3 — IMPERIAL DOLPHIN | 12.00-14.00 | Single |
| 4 & 5 — EMPIRE DOLPHIN | 16.00-20.00 | Pair |

BOTTOM ROW

| | | |
|---|---|---|
| 1 & 3 — "NEWBOUND" PATTERN 153B | 24.00-30.00 | Pair |
| 2 — PATTERN 637 (Gold Overlay) | 28.00-30.00 | Single |

## PLATE XXII

TOP ROW

| | | |
|---|---|---|
| 1 & 2 — SPECIAL LOT PATTERN NO. 41 | 22.00-28.00 | Pair |

MIDDLE ROW

| | | |
|---|---|---|
| 1 — PATTERN NO. 419 | 28.00-34.00 | Single |
| 2 — PATTERN NO. 419 | 30.00-38.00 | Single |

BOTTOM ROW

| | | |
|---|---|---|
| 1 & 4 — PATTERN NO. 635 | 42.00-46.00 | Pair |
| 2 — PATTERN NO. 635 | 28.00-30.00 | Single |
| 3 — PATTERN NO. 635 | 18.00-24.00 | Single |

## PLATE XXIII

TOP ROW

| | | |
|---|---|---|
| 1 — GARLAND NO. 301 Line | 15.00-18.00 | Single |

BOTTOM ROW

| | | |
|---|---|---|
| 1 & 3 — SANDWICH PATTERN NO. 41 | 14.00-16.00 | Pair |
| 2 — EARLY AMERICAN PATTERN NO. 170 | 12.00-14.00 | Single |

## PLATE XXIV

TOP ROW

| | | |
|---|---|---|
| 1 & 3 — PATTERN NO. 26 | 35.00-40.00 | Single |
| 2 — PATTERN NO. 26 | 25.00-30.00 | Single |

MIDDLE ROW

| | | |
|---|---|---|
| PATTERN NO. X-31 (Average) | 8.00-14.00 | Single |
| | 18.00-22.00 | Pair |

BOTTOM ROW

1, 2 & 3 — IRIS

| | | |
|---|---|---|
| FROSTED | 10.00-12.00 | Single |
| CLEAR CRYSTAL | 7.00-9.00 | Single |
| IRIDESCENT | 10.00-12.00 | Single |

## PLATE XXV

*TOP ROW*
1 & 3 — PATTERN NO. 854 . . . . . . . . . . . . . .      6.00-8.00   Pair
2 — PATTERN NO. R-1830 . . . . . . . . . . .      3.00-4.00   Single
*MIDDLE ROW*
1 & 3 — PATTERN NO. 83 . . . . . . . . . . . . . .      8.00-10.00   Single
2 — PATTERN NO. 83 . . . . . . . . . . . . . .      8.00-10.00   Single
*BOTTOM ROW*
1, 2 & 3 — PATTERN NO. 83 SET . . . . . . . . . . . .      35.00-40.00   Set

## PLATE XXVI

*TOP ROW*
1 — VULCAN DESIGN . . . . . . . . . . . . . .      12.00-14.00   Single
2 — SMALL CRUCIFIX . . . . . . . . . . . . .      28.00-30.00   Single
*BOTTOM ROW*
1 & 2 — RAY . . . . . . . . . . . . . . . . . . . . . . . . . .      48.00-52.00   Pair

## PLATE XXVII

1 — CANDELABRA . . . . . . . . . . . . . . . . . .      100.00-125.00   Single
2 — BOY WITH HORN-OF-PLENTY . . .      125.00-145.00   Single

## PLATE XXVIII

*TOP ROW*
1 & 2 — PATTERN NO. 415 . . . . . . . . . . . . . .      25.00-30.00   Pair
*MIDDLE ROW*
1 & 3 — PATTERN NO. 10 . . . . . . . . . . . . . .      9.00-12.00   Pair
2 — PATTERN NO. 10 . . . . . . . . . . . . . .      4.00-6.00   Single
*BOTTOM ROW*
1 & 3 — VOGUE PATTERN NO. 4554/401 . .      20.00-22.00   Pair
2 — PATTERN NO. 18 . . . . . . . . . . . . . .      10.00-14.00   Single

## PLATE XXIX

*TOP ROW*
1 & 2 — PATTERN NO. 169 . . . . . . . . . . . . . .      14.00-18.00   Pair
*MIDDLE ROW*
1 & 2 — PATTERN NO. 14 . . . . . . . . . . . . . .      32.00-36.00   Pair
*BOTTOM ROW*
1 & 3 — COLONIAL — PATTERN NO. 11 . .      16.00-18.00   Pair
2 — PATTERN NO. 19 . . . . . . . . . . . . . .      8.00-10.00   Single

## PLATE XXX

*TOP ROW*
1 — AIR TWIST . . . . . . . . . . . . . . . . . . . .      75.00-85.00   Single
*MIDDLE ROW*
1 — SWIRL BALL . . . . . . . . . . . . . . . . . . . .      36.00-40.00   Single
2 — BELL TOP . . . . . . . . . . . . . . . . . . . . . .      25.00-35.00   Single
3 — SILVER BASE . . . . . . . . . . . . . . . . . .      30.00-34.00   Single
*BOTTOM ROW*
1, 2 & 3 — AMBER BOWL SET . . . . . . . . . . . . . .      85.00-95.00   Set

## PLATE XXXI

*TOP ROW*
1 — COCK'S FOOT AND LEG . . . . . . . . .      15.00-18.00   Single
2 — DRAGON . . . . . . . . . . . . . . . . . . . . .      18.00-22.00   Single
*MIDDLE ROW*
1 — COCK'S FOOT — EGG SENTER . .      65.00-75.00   Single
2 — COCK'S FOOT — EGG CENTER . .      65.00-75.00   Single
*BOTTOM ROW*
1 — COCK'S FOOT — GLASS CENTER      60.00-70.00   Single
2 — OAK LEAVES WITH GLASS . . . . . .      90.00-100.00   Single
3 — COCK'S FOOT AND GLASS . . . . . .      100.00-125.00   Single

## PLATE XXXII

*TOP ROW*

1 — MONK . . . . . . . . . . . . . . . . . . . . . . . .     35.00-40.00   Single

*BOTTOM ROW*

1 & 2 — DRUNK AROUND LAMP POST . .     70.00-80.00   Pair

## PLATE XXXIII

1 & 2 — ROSENTHAL TULIPS . . . . . . . . . . .     200.00-225.00

## PLATE XXXIV

*TOP ROW*

1 & 2 — MOUNT PLEASANT — PATTERN
NO. 600 . . . , . . . . . . . . . . . . . . . . . .     18.00-22.00   Pair

*MIDDLE ROW*

1 & 2 — CRYSTAL MOLDED
WITH PRISMS . . . . . . . . . . . . . . .     35.00-40.00   Pair

*BOTTOM ROW*

1 & 4 — PATTERN NO. 805 . . . . . . . . . . . . . .     14.00-18.00   Pair

2 & 3 — CRUCIFIX . . . . . . . . . . . . . . . . . . . . .     40.00-50.00   Pair

## PLATE XXXV

*TOP ROW*

1 — BLUE COLUMN . . . . . . . . . . . . . . . .     45.00-55.00   Single

2 — BLUE HOUR-GLASS . . . . . . . . . . . .     60.00-70.00   Single

*MIDDLE ROW*

1 — CRYSTAL . . . . . . . . . . . . . . . . . . . . . .     75.00-85.00   Single

1, 2 & 3 — YELLOW BOWL SET . . . . . . . . . . . .     250.00-300.00   Set

## PLATE XXXVI

*TOP ROW*

1 — PATTERN NO. 6043 . . . . . . . . . . . . . .     100.00-125.00   Single

2 — PATTERN NO. 6505 . . . . . . . . . . . . . .     145.00-165.00   Single

*BOTTOM ROW*

1 — PATTERN NO. 6384 . . . . . . . . . . . . . .     40.00-50.00   Single

2 & 3 — PATTERN NO. 2956 . . . . . . . . . . . . . .     300.00-325.00   Pair

4 — PATTERN NO. 2940 . . . . . . . . . . . . . .     60.00-65.00   Single

## PLATE XXXVII

*TOP ROW*

1 & 2 — PATTERN NO. 15319 . . . . . . . . . . . . .     38.00-42.00   Pair

*MIDDLE ROW*

1, 2 & 3 — ELYSIUM . . . . . . . . . . . . . . . . . . . . . .     6.00-8.00   Single

*BOTTOM ROW*

1, 2 & 3 — BLACK TIFFIN GLASS . . . . . . . . . .     45.00-50.00   Set

## PLATE XXXVIII

*TOP ROW*

1 — DOLPHINS . . . . . . . . . . . . . . . . . . . . .     75.00-85.00   Single

*BOTTOM ROW*

1 — DOLPHIN . . . . . . . . . . . . . . . . . . . . .     40.00-45.00   Single

2 — ROSES . . . . . . . . . . . . . . . . . . . . . . . .     50.00-60.00   Single

3 — VASA MURRHINA . . . . . . . . . . . . .     42.00-48.00   Single

## PLATE XXXIX

*TOP ROW*

1 — PATTERN NO. 1049
DOLPHIN . . . . . . . . . . . . . . . . . . . .     10.00-12.00   Single

2 & 3 — PATTERN NO. 1049
MILK GLASS DOLPHIN . . . . . . .     6.00-8.00   Pair
(If new)

*BOTTOM ROW*

1 & 2 — CRYSTAL DOLPHIN . . . . . . . . . . . .     60.00-70.00   Pair

PLATE XXXX

*TOP ROW*
    1 — LOTUS — SATIN AMBER ........    10.00-12.00  Single
*MIDDLE ROW*
    1 — CLEAR WITH ORANGE AND
        BLACK ......................    15.00-17.00  Single
    2 — PATTERN NO. 1803
        GREEN SATIN ...............    18.00-20.00  Single
    3 — PINK WITH BLACK BASE .......    15.00-17.00  Single
*BOTTOM ROW*
    1 & 3 — PATTERN NO. 1803 ..............    30.00-32.00  Pair
    2 — PATTERN NO. 1803 .............    18.00-20.00  Single

PLATE XXXXI

*TOP ROW*
    1 — FEDERAL'S FLUTE .............    9.00-11.00  Single
*MIDDLE ROW*
    1 — GREENBURG'S PATTERN 1402 ..    6.00-7.00  Single
    2 — HAZEL ATLAS DOLPHIN ........    18.00-20.00  Single
*BOTTOM ROW*
    1 — GORHAM'S "THE TWLIGHT —
        PATENTED" .................    40.00-50.00  Single

PLATE XXXXII

*TOP ROW*
    1 — PADEN CITY...................    6.00-8.00  Single
    2 — PHOENIX .....................    28.00-32.00  Single
*MIDDLE ROW*
        NO VALUE LISTED
*BOTTOM ROW*
        NO VALUE LISTED

UNKNOWNS
NO VALUE LISTED